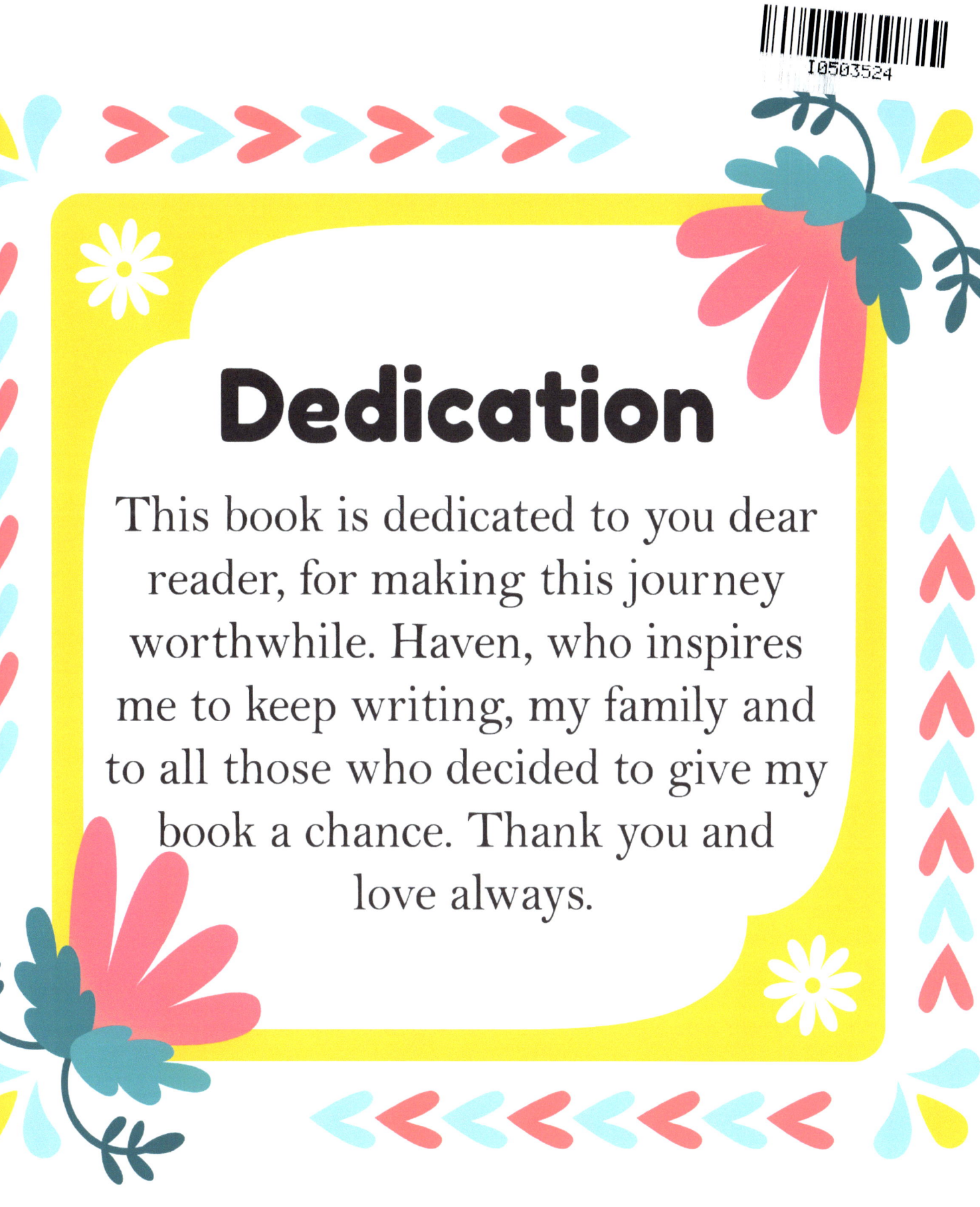

# Dedication

This book is dedicated to you dear reader, for making this journey worthwhile. Haven, who inspires me to keep writing, my family and to all those who decided to give my book a chance. Thank you and love always.

Mom what is a superhero?
Asked Theo
Mom replied
Superheroes are people like
me and you!

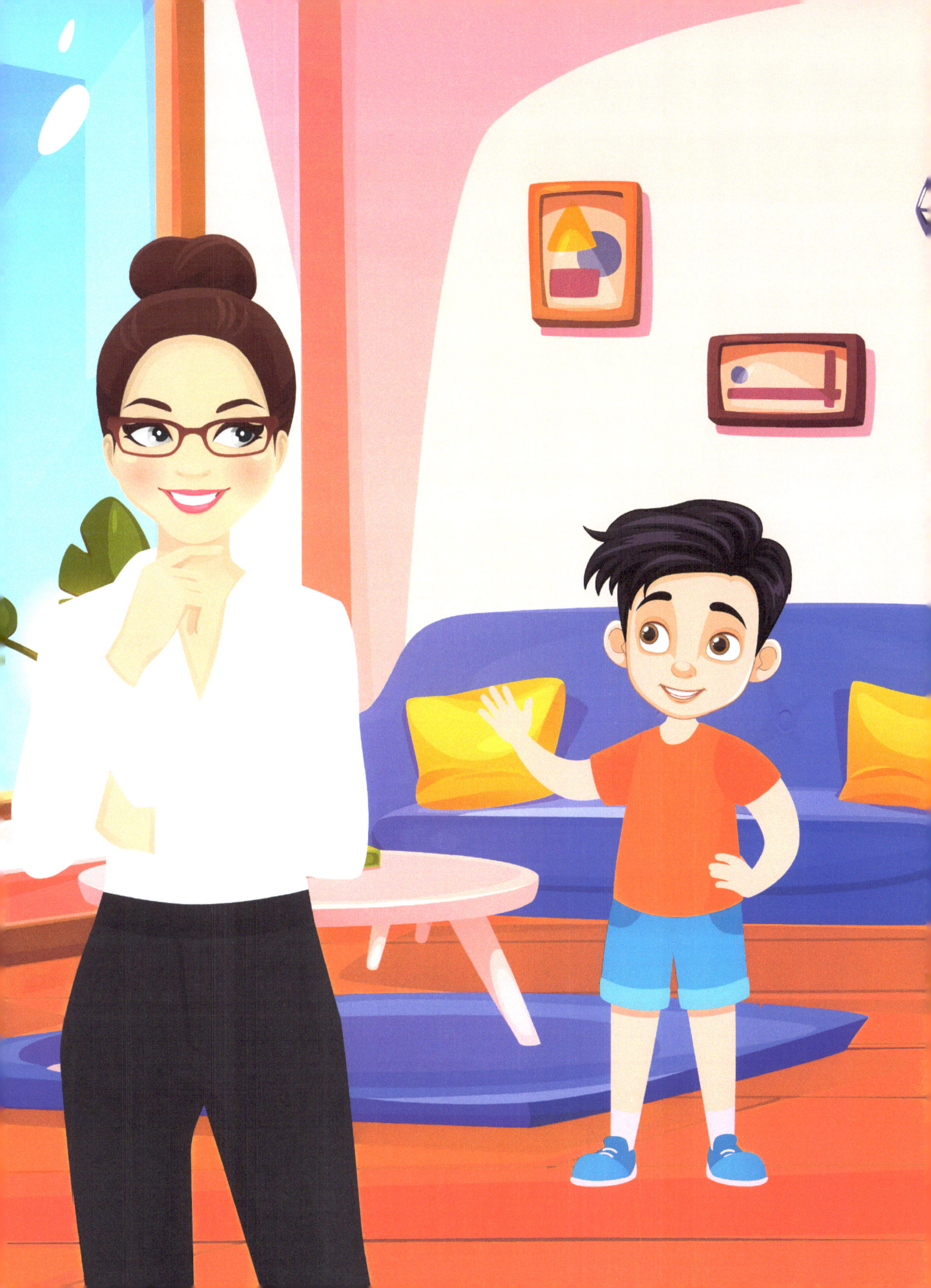

You see, mom went on to explain
A superhero is a doctor like Jane who cares for the sick!
And lovingly reminds you to take your medication when the clock ticks!

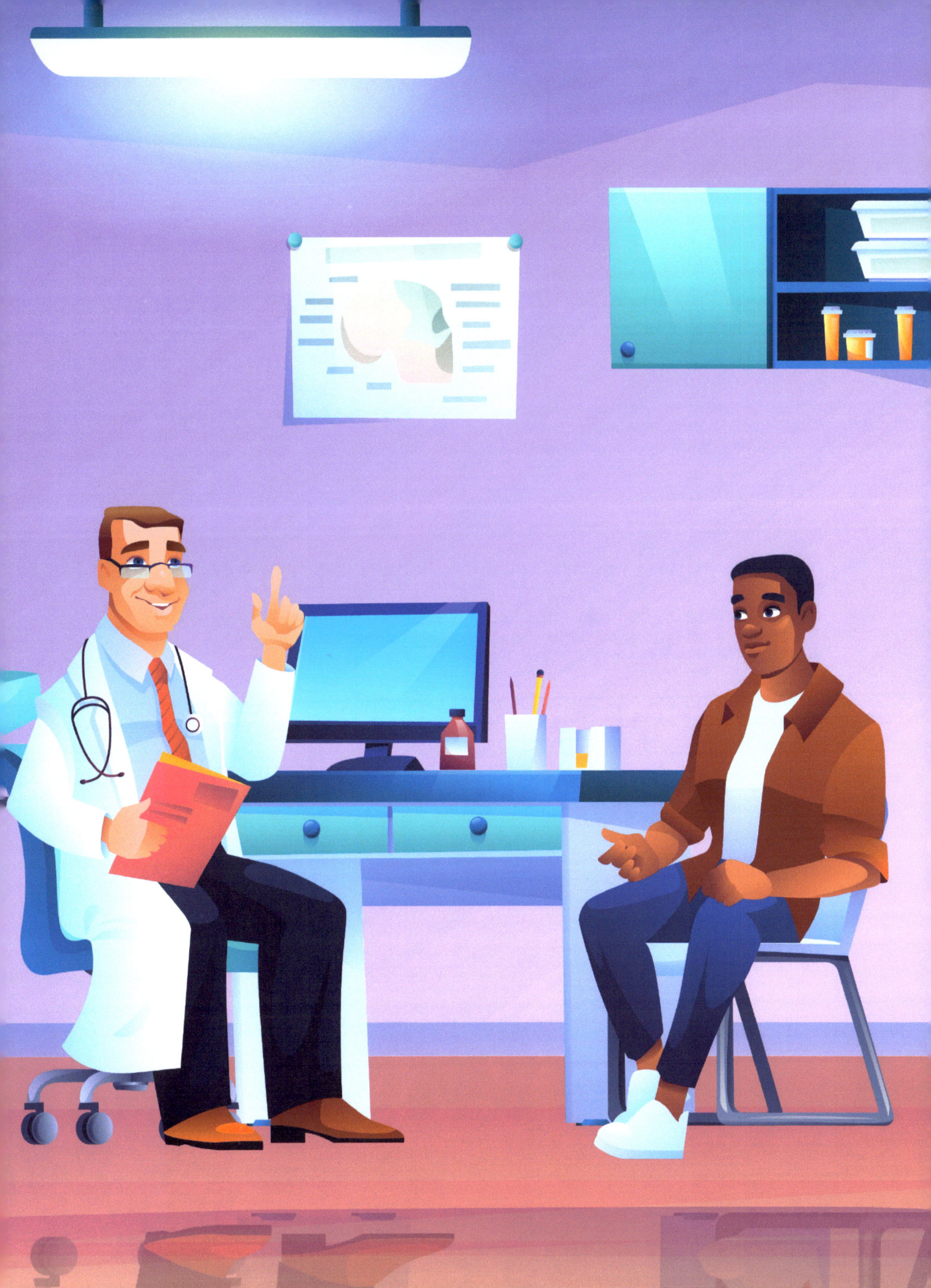

A superhero is a Firefighter just like Dave.
Who helps put out the fire and ensures everyone is safe!

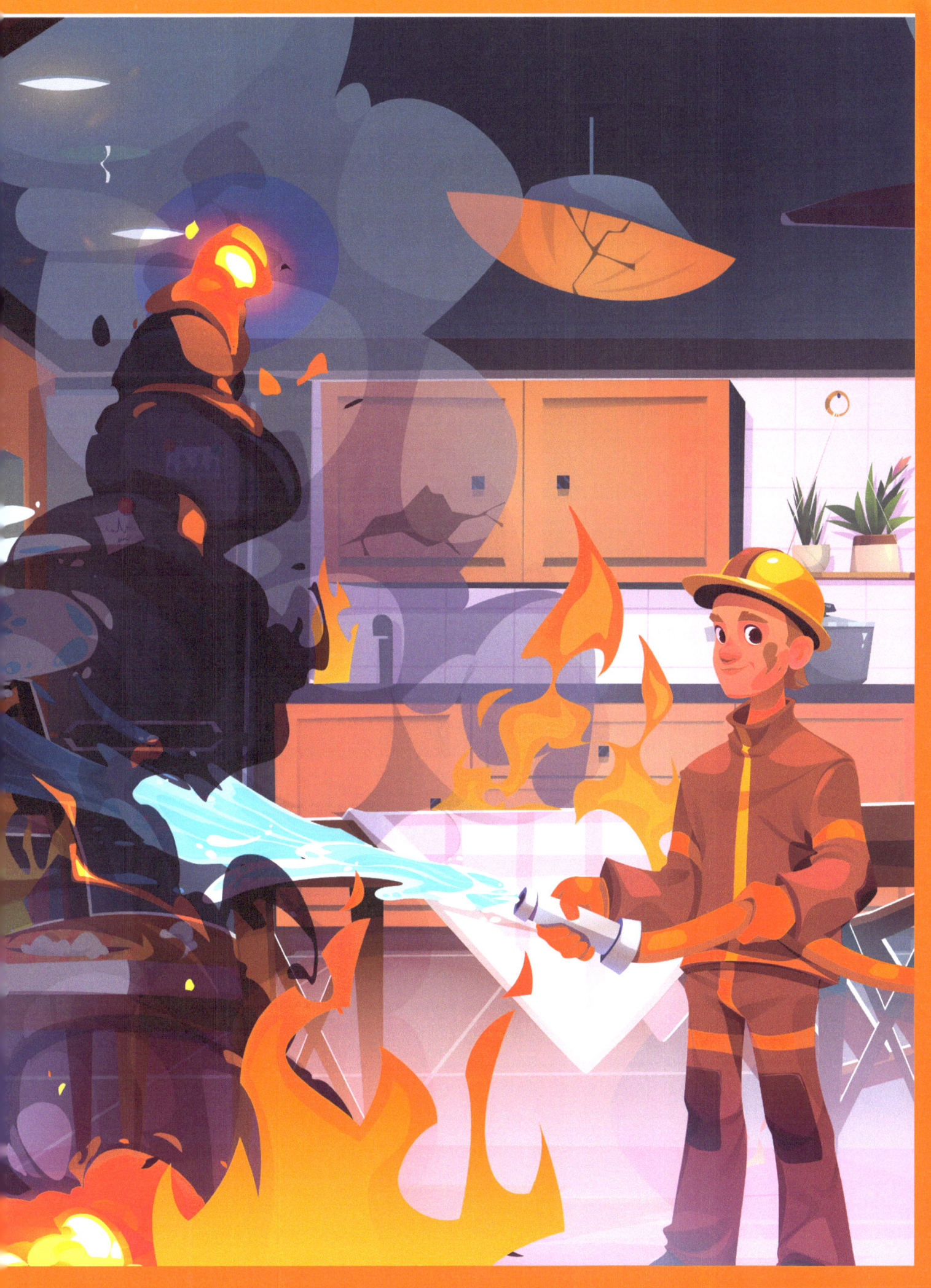

A superhero is Andy the vet
He comes in handy
When caring for sick pets.

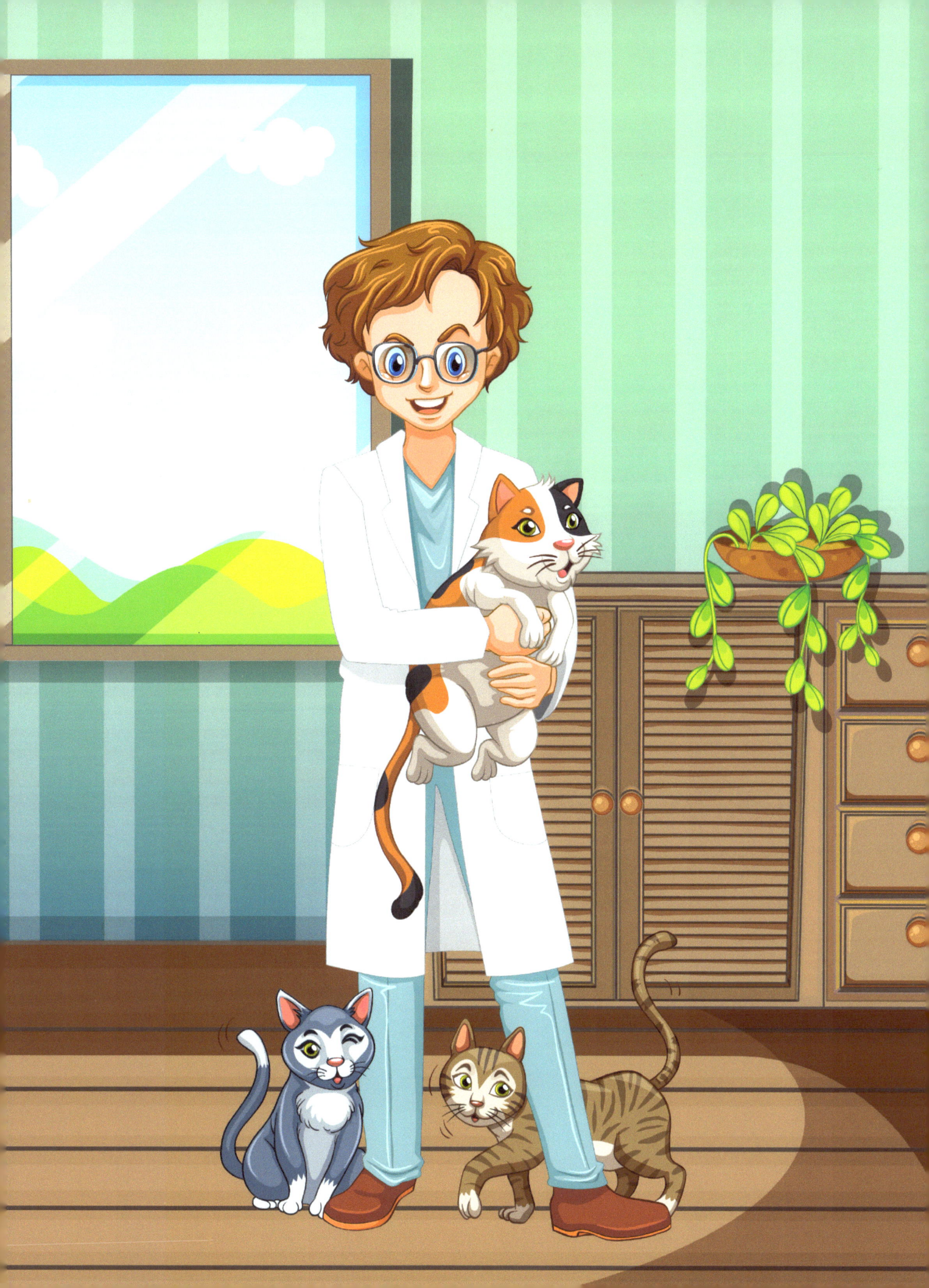

A superhero is a teacher
Like Miss Alexander –
Samuel
Who helps students to read
and spell!
Now Theo, can you tell me
of some other superheroes?

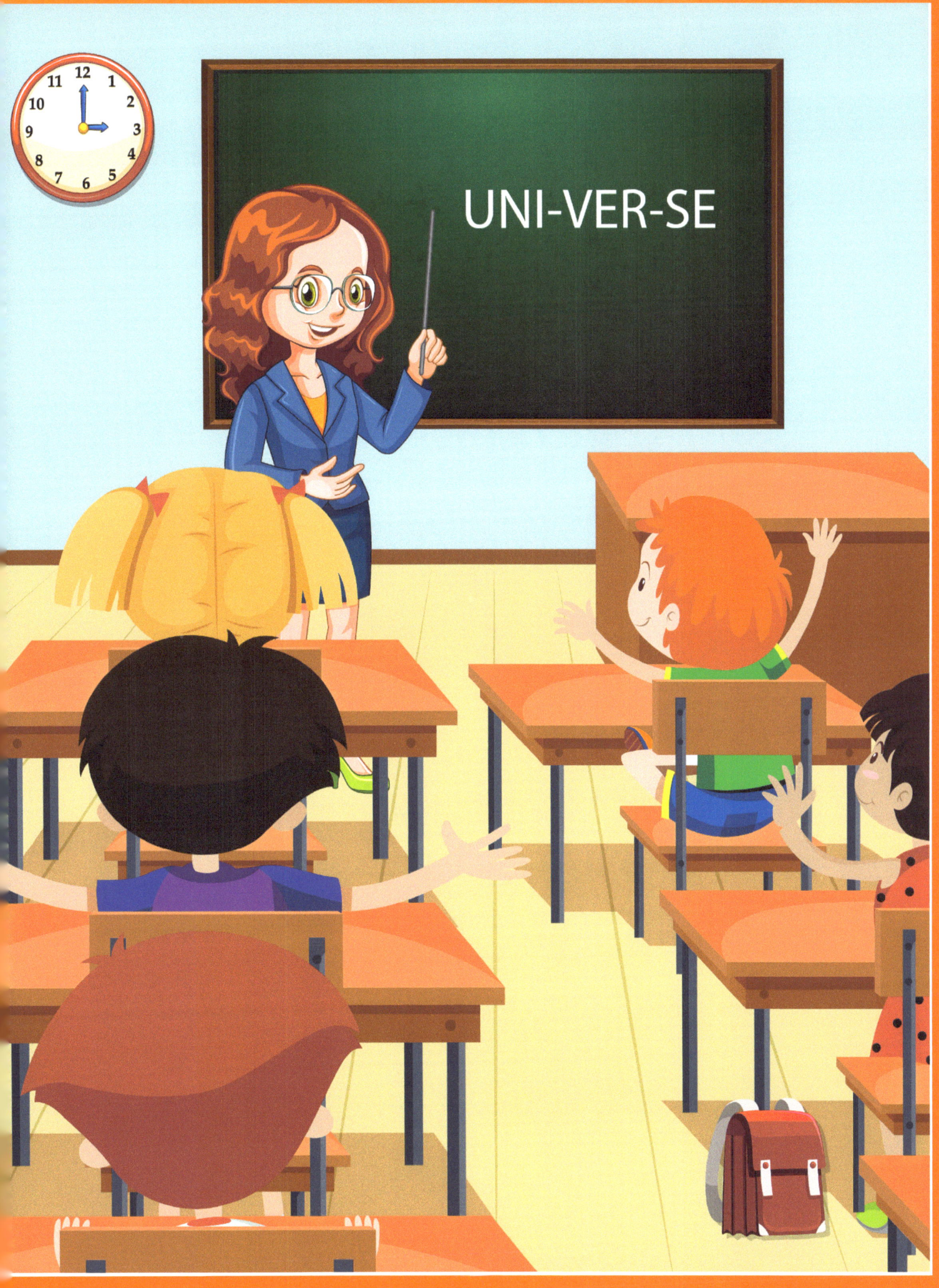

A superhero is Clyde the police man
Who makes sure to protect and serve!
Bringing justice when people do us wrong
And peace to troubled communities all over town.

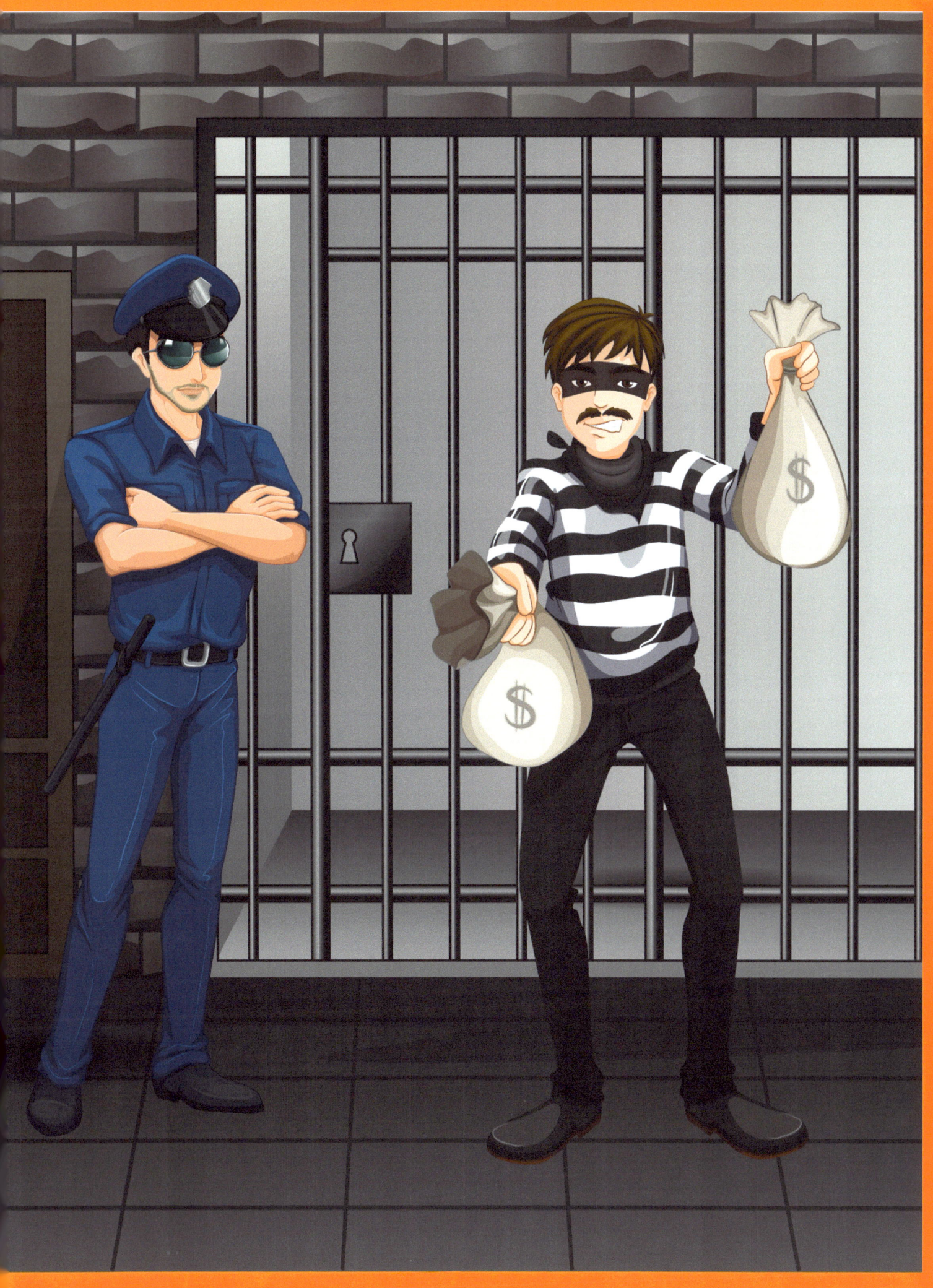

Mom you see,
A superhero is a person like
Aunt Gabby.
She rescued a bird that fell from
a tree.
Nice Theo,
Can you go on?
Yes mom, but the list is long
Ok, Theo tell me more!

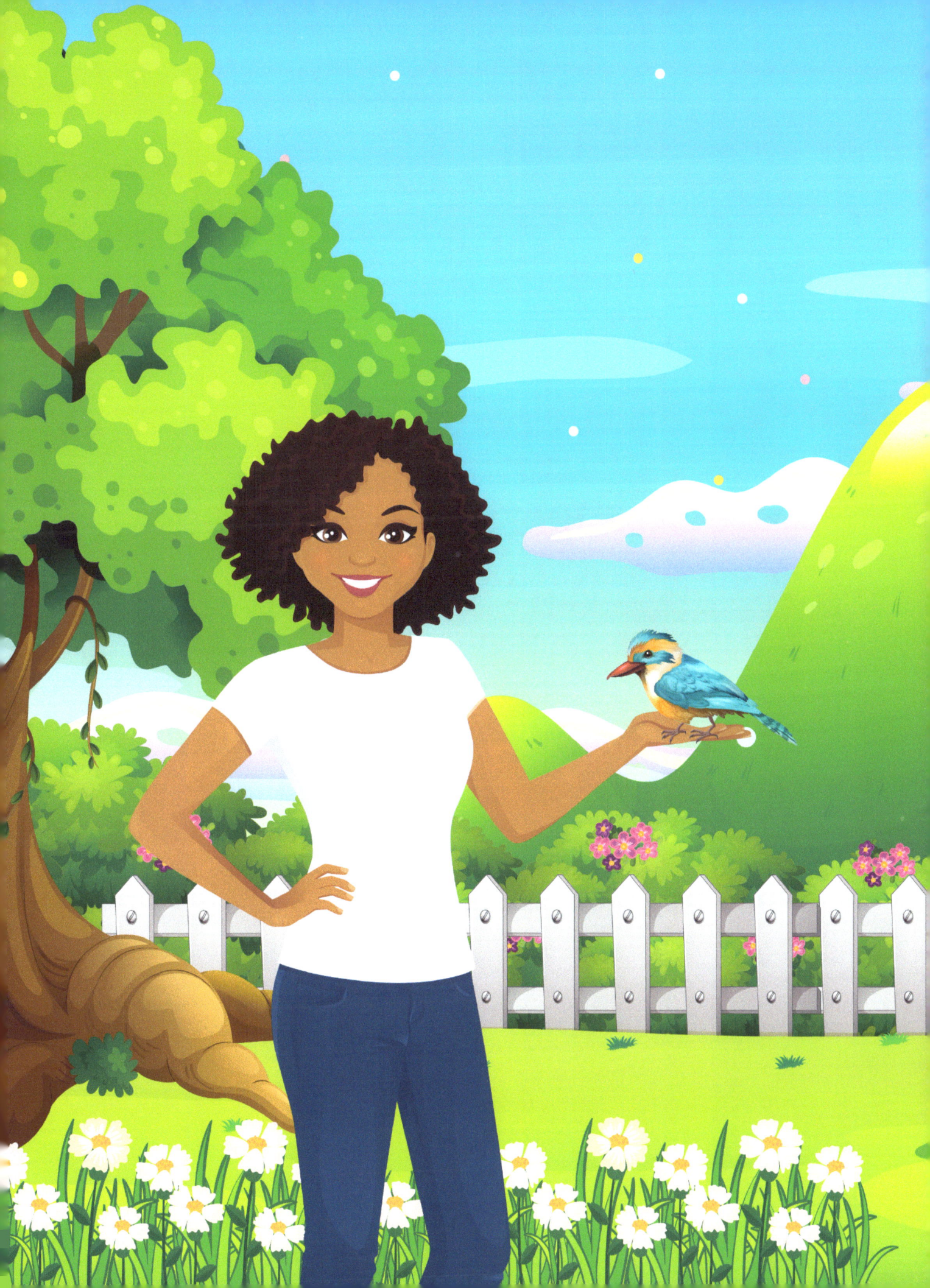

Mom a superhero is me too
Because I always feed the poor.
Yes Theo, that is quite true
You are indeed a superhero
And I am so proud of you.

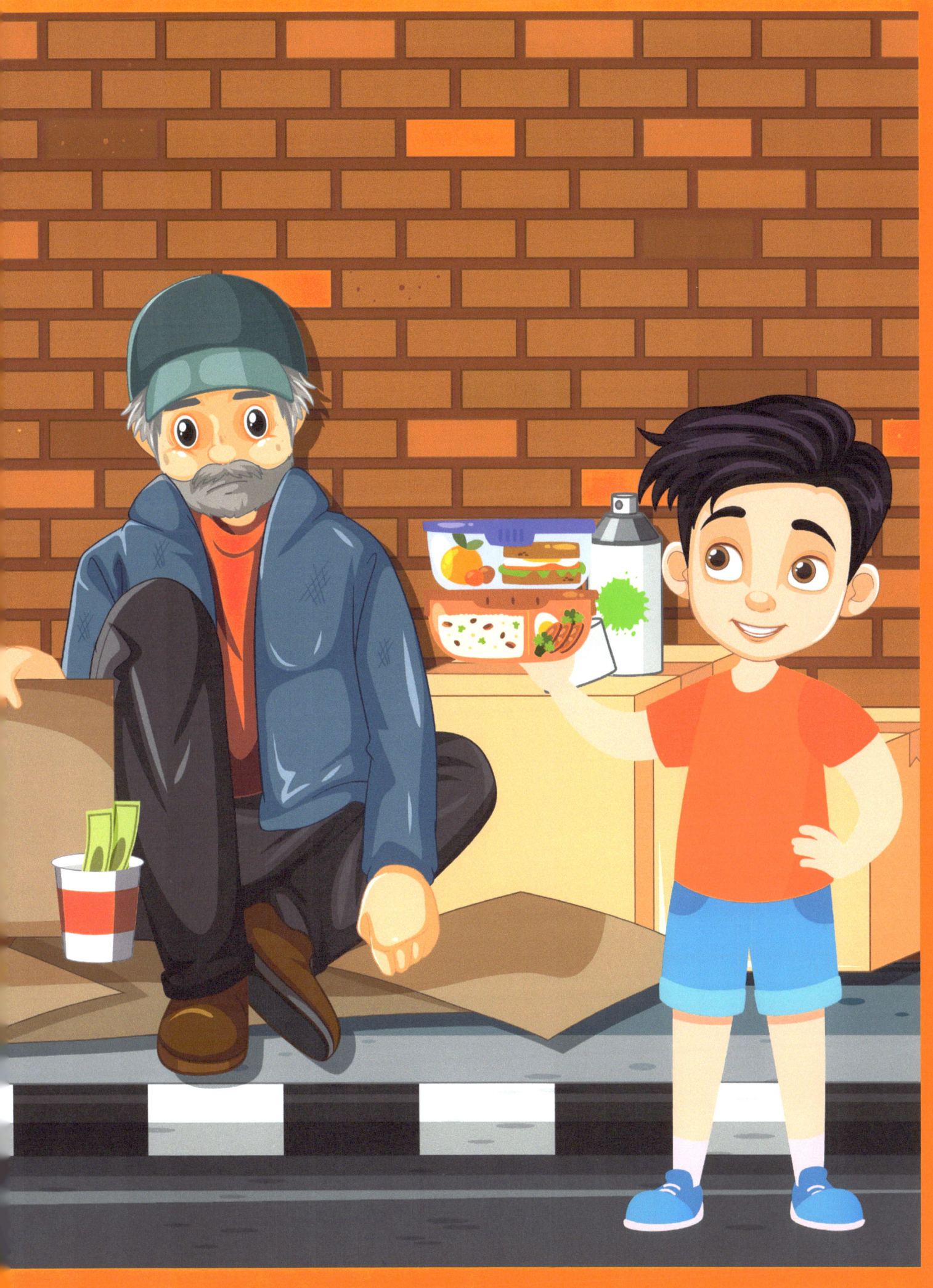

A superhero is anyone who is kind as you.
Daddy Corrie is also a superhero,
He fix all the pipe lines when it is burst.
As quick as possible before it gets worse.

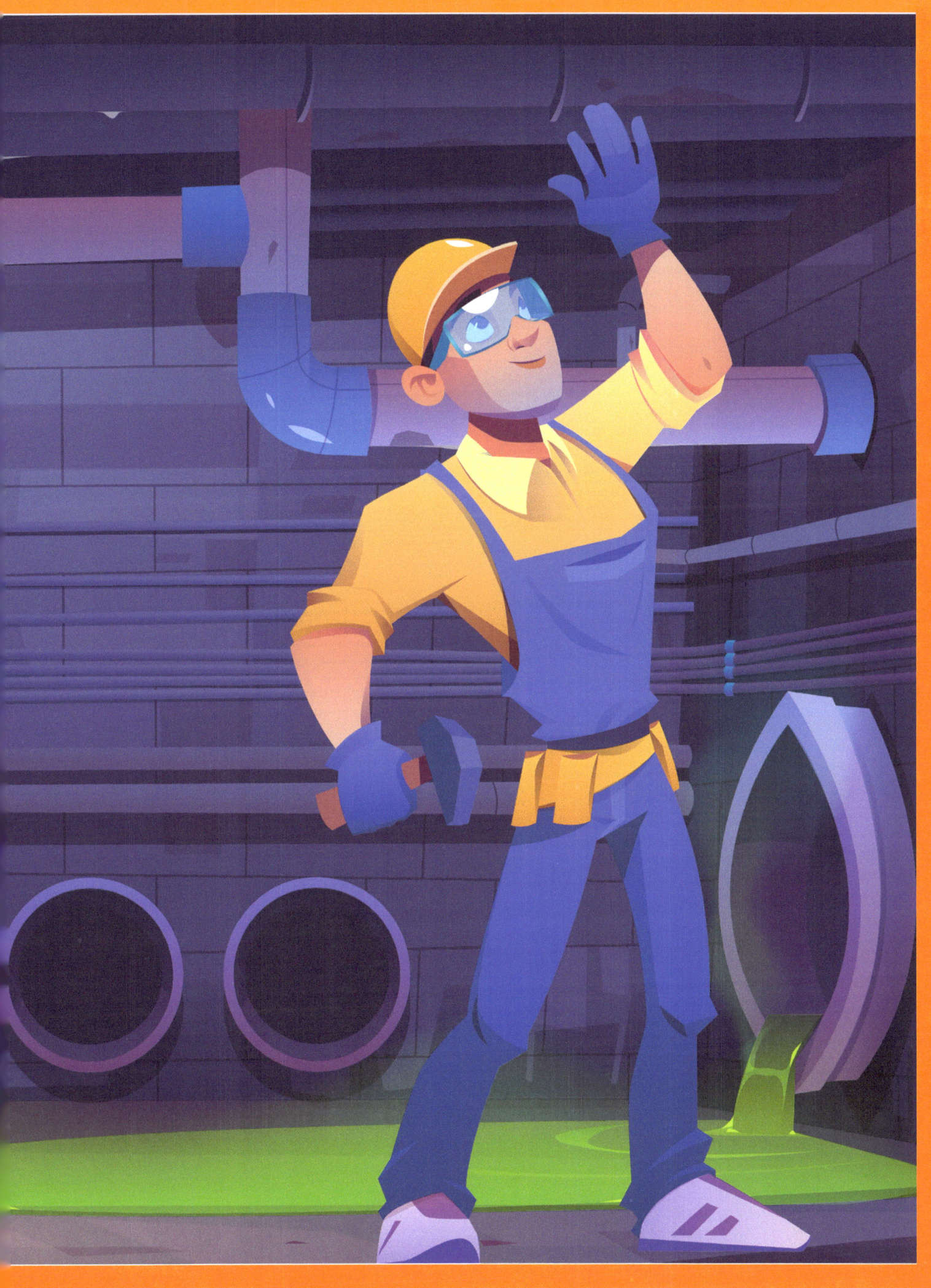

And don't forget the garbage disposal man!
No, Theo I can't!
They help keep our neighborhood tidy
From overflowing rubbish in our trash cans.

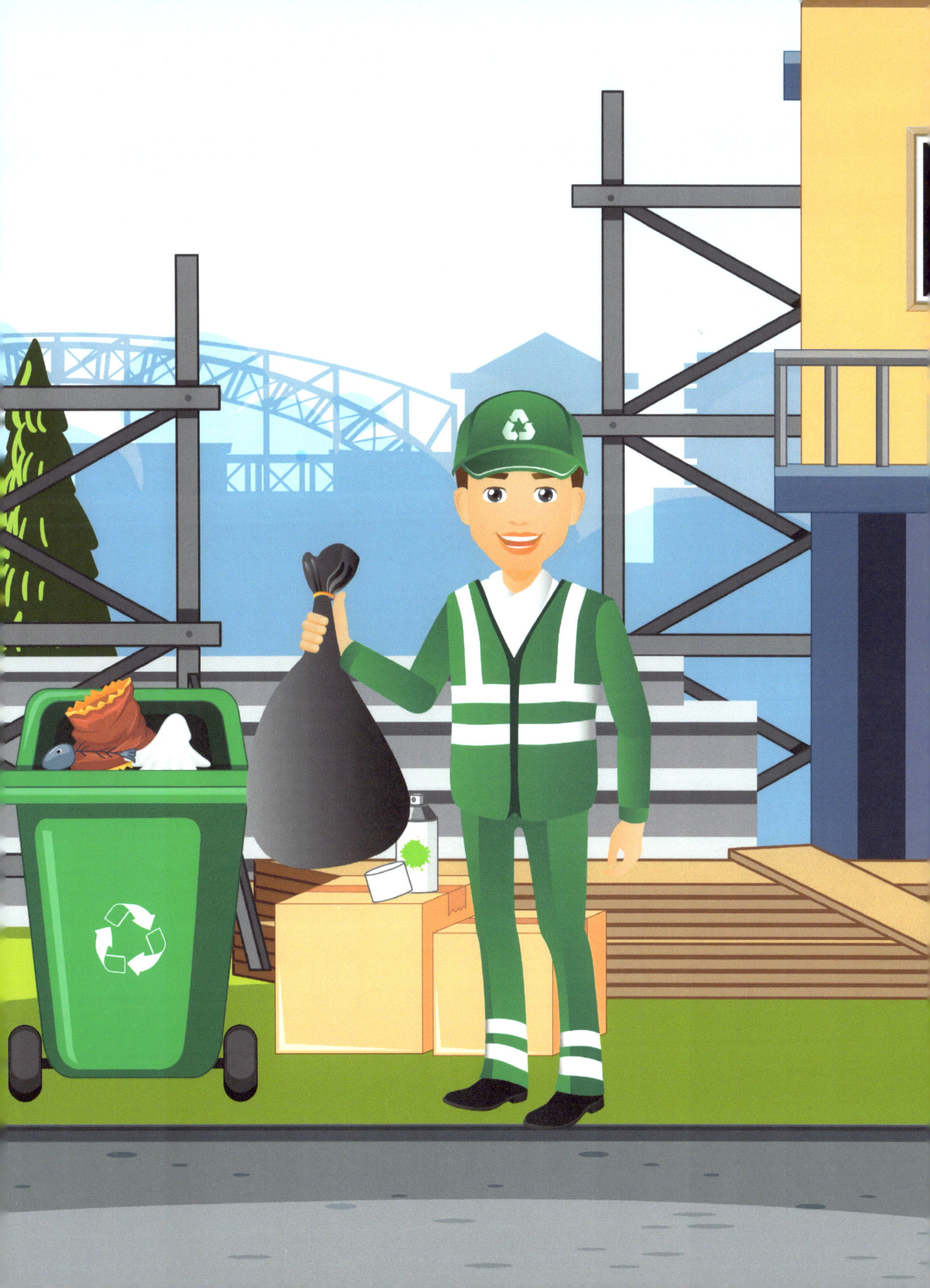

A superhero is Joe the life guard.
Who is always alert
Watching out for others at the
beach so they won't get hurt.
He is quick to jump in and rescue
When he sees danger near you.

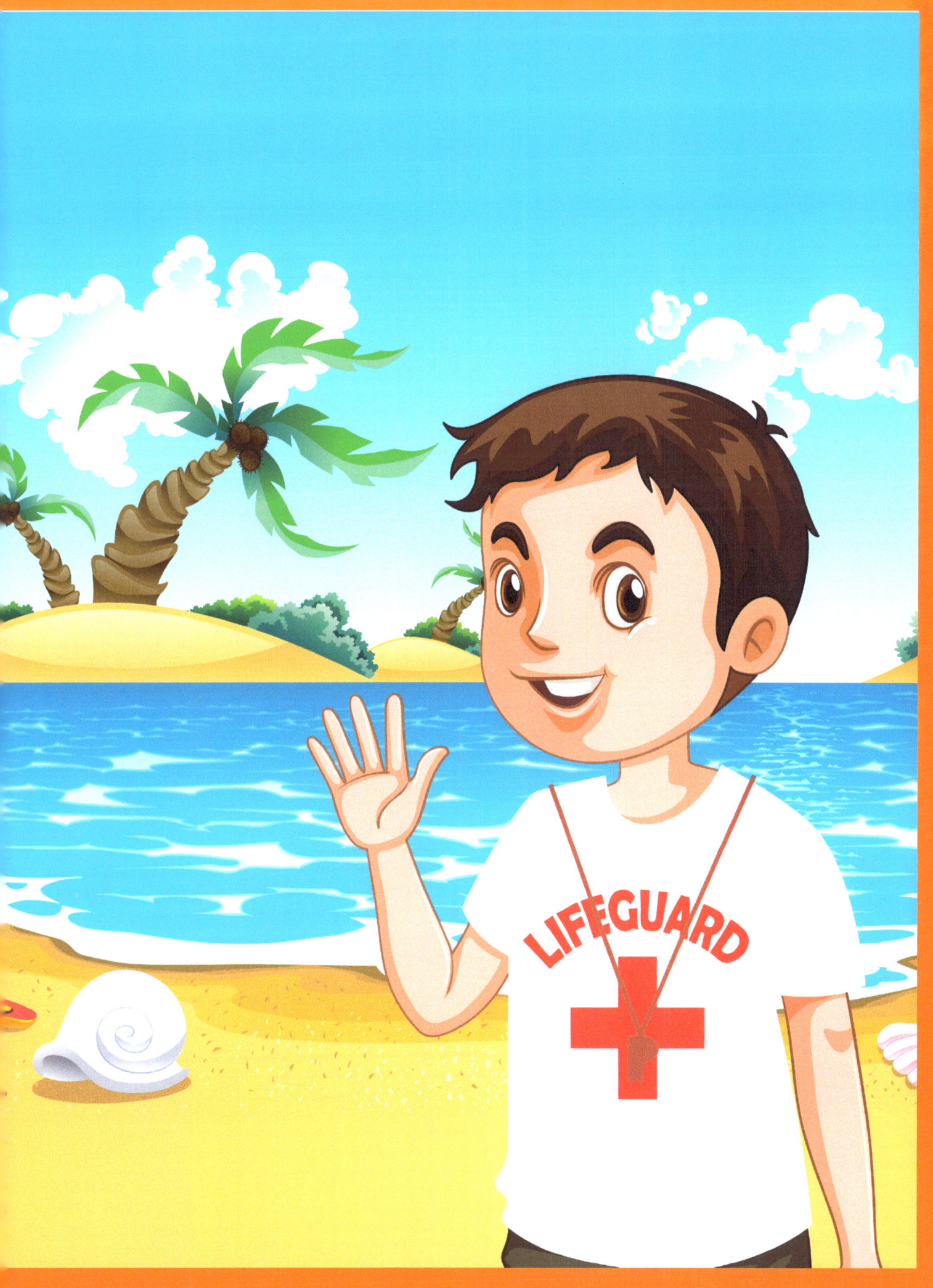

So you see, Theo a superhero is anyone with a kind heart. Making this world so beautiful to be apart

So Theo, just like you
A superhero is anybody
Whose heart is pure and true.

So love everyone and treat them well.
Because you do not know when you may need their help.

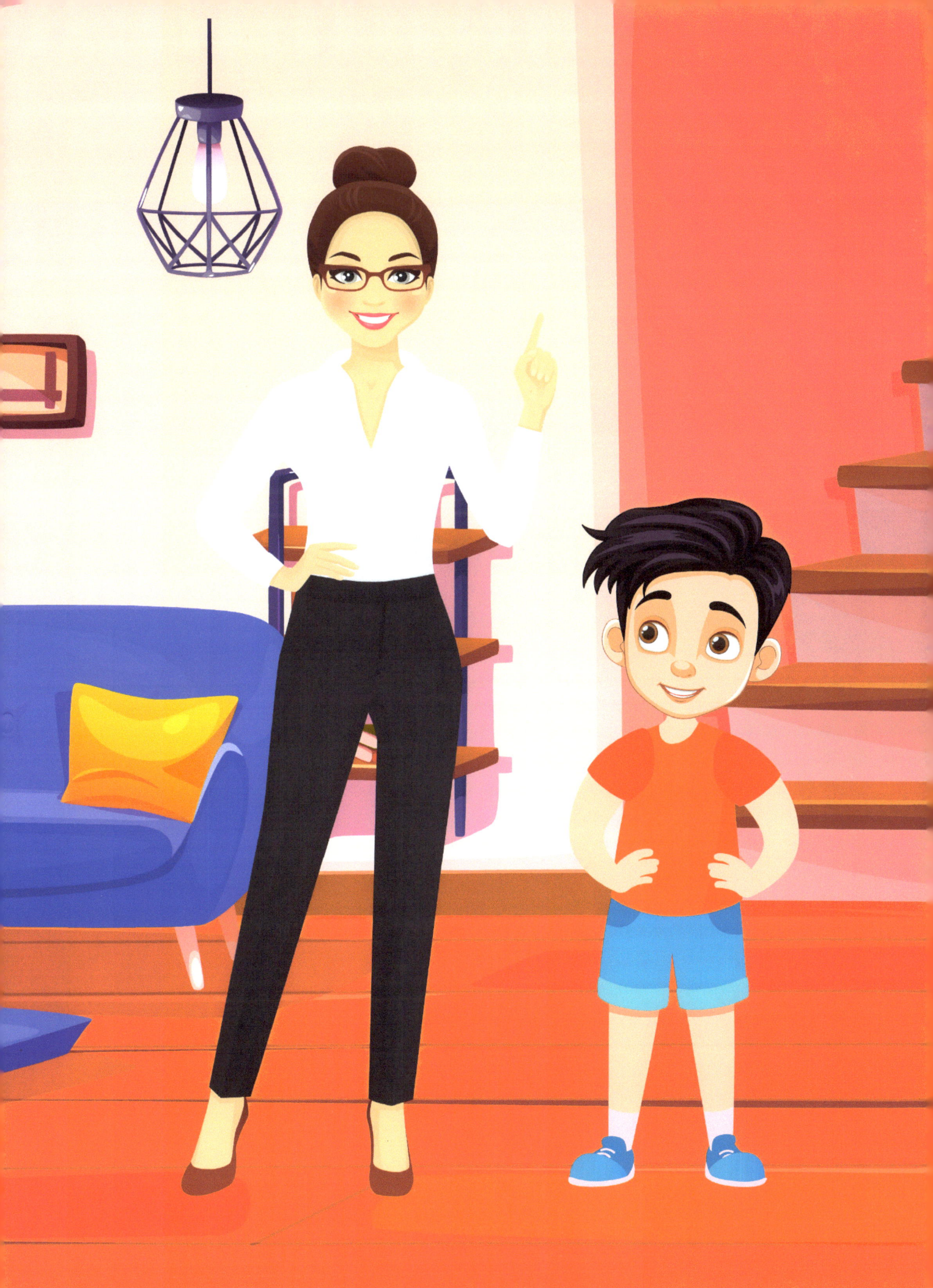

So superheroes is not only who we see on tv.
But they are people we see quite daily.

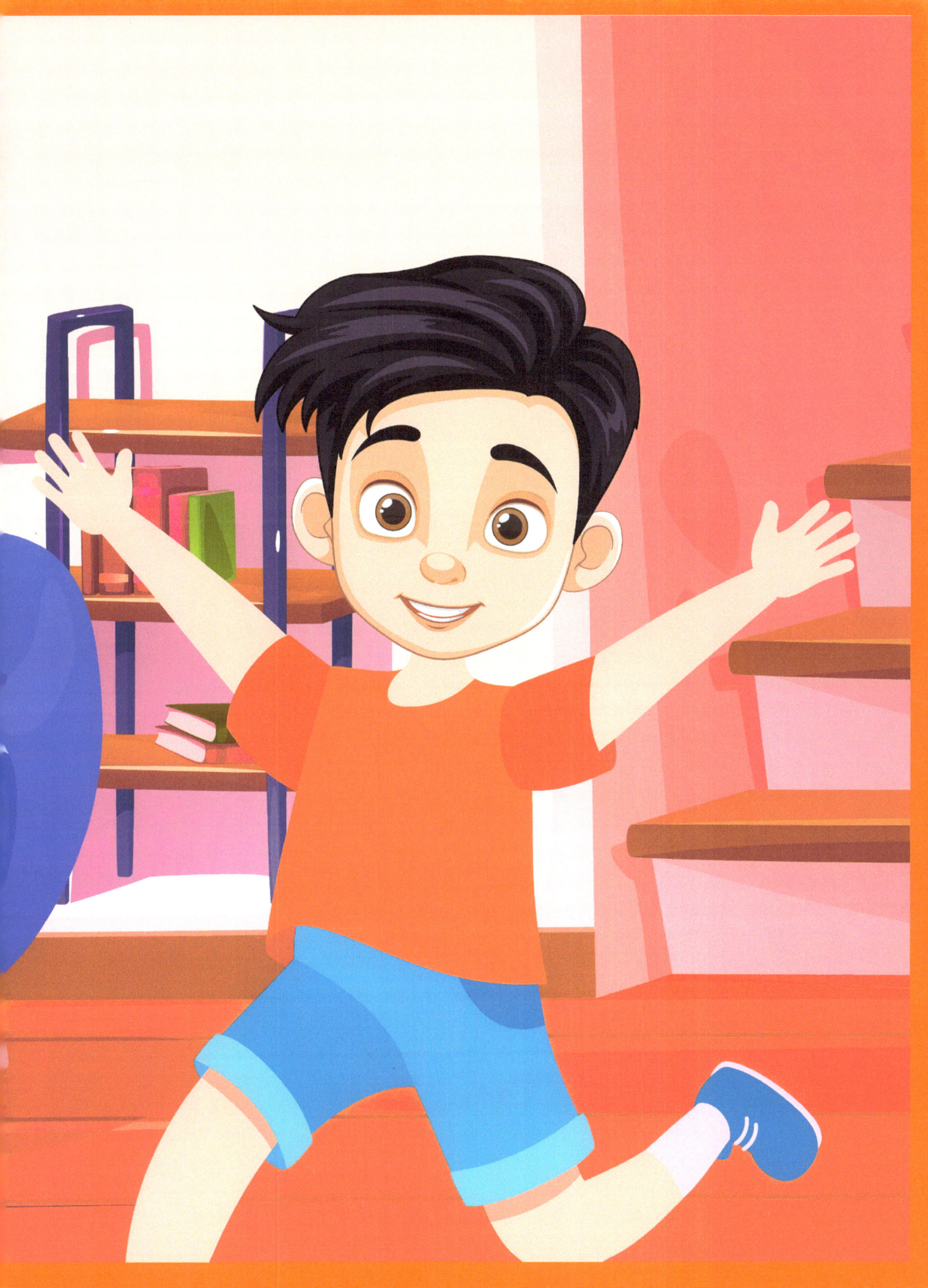